TO: Mrs. Ware

EVERYBODY CAN'T BE A STAR, SOMEBODY HAS TO APPLAUD

A FAMOUS QUOTE
FROM
THE LATE MR. RUDOLPH LIPSEY SR.

Thank you, and God Bless

R. Lipsey

I GIVE ALL PRAISE TO GOD

UPLIFTING POEMS
FOR TROUBLED HEARTS

THE GRATEFUL POET
BY RUDOLPH LIPSEY
(TAMIR)

**UPLIFTING POEMS PUBLISHING
NEWARK, NJ
(THE BRICK CITY)**

Library of Congress TXU-152-843
Printing in the UNITED STATES OF AMERICA

First Printing
UPLIFTING POEMS FOR
TROUBLED HEARTS

Published by Uplifting Poems Publishing

Cover design and layout by *Tracy C. Lipsey*

For information or to order additional books, please
write:
Uplifting Poems Publishing
P. O. BOX 13155
Jersey City, NJ 07303
RUDOLPHLIPSEY@HOTMAIL.COM

MY BOOK

I wanted to write a book for the whole world to read
A book that will reach those who are in desperate need

Teach our children about God's mercy and grace
Showing them the cultural difference in each particular race

My book defines life, peace, joy, happiness, and love
The five qualities passed down from up above

My book is to let the world know that life is a good thing
Whether it's summer, winter, autumn or spring

The best things in life are faith and sharing
It exemplifies the true meaning of loving and caring

When you read my book your heart will be at ease
Your soul will become excited and extremely pleased

I will tell stories you may have heard before
Deliver a message to the rich and the poor

When you open my book it will be difficult to close
Every page you read is like a flower that grows

DEDICATION, IN MEMORY

I DEDICATE MY BOOK TO MY PARENTS THE LATE MR. RUDOLPH LIPSEY SR. / MRS. WILLIE B. LIPSEY MAY THEY R.I.P., MY MOTHER IN-LAW MRS. SHIRLEY P. PURNELL, MY AUNTS SULENA, BETTY, MY GRANDMOTHER MRS. JESSIE B. LEE, THE CHIEF, UNCLE LEO, AUNT JOHNNIE TYRONE, ROGER, JAMEEL, RAHEEM, BILLY, RASHAD, GREAT-GRAND-MOTHER, MRS. IRENE BRITTAN, BIG AKBAR, WALI-VIC, UNCLE BIGMAN, GRANDMA PURNELL, GRANDMA OGLATHA WILLIAMS, COUSIN JET, VALERIE, JUDY, ANN, COUSIN ANNA, JASON, LEAH GREEN, COUSIN LULU, HAKIM, AUNT GATHERINE, AND OTIS WILLIAMS.

ACKNOWLEDGEMENTS

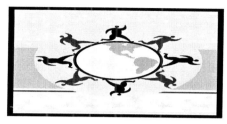

SPECIAL THANKS TO MY LOVELY WIFE

TRACY LIPSEY WHO SUPPORTED ME IN WRITING THIS BOOK OF POEMS, TO MY CHILDREN, MANISA, TAQUAN, SAMIRA, MY SISTERS NANCY LEE, ELIZABETH LEE, EILEEN KIRKLAND, DENISE CREEKMUR, ALTHEA LIPSEY, AUNT BETTY, MY FATHER IN-LAW WILLIAM PURNELL, SHALEEN, SHIRLEY, & DIRENE PURNELL, BROTHER-LAWS BILL, CHARLIE, JOHN, INNOCENT, MY GRANDMOTHER JOAN THOMAS, AUNT IRENE, TAWANDA THOMAS, UNCLE JIMMY, STANLEY, AUNTS SIS & STEPHANIE, UNCLE KIRK WILLIAMS, CASSANDRA HEMBY, PAULA WILLIAMS, UNCLE JOSEPH PURNELL, KEVIN THOMAS, KELVIN TAYLOR, JAMAL AND MELVINA PEARSON, CASSANDRA MUHAMMAD, SERENA INGRAM CYNTHIA, & PRISCILLA TAYLOR, NIECES NANETTE, JYVETTE, REGINA, VENUS, TRINA LEE, LAKEYAH PURNELL, DEANNA CREEKMUR, TAYSIA LIPSEY, NEPHEWS TALEEL, KHALIL, TAMIR, JOHN, SHERROD, COUSINS HASSAN LEE, ADAM WILLIAMS, UNCLE TICK, HERMAN, FARAD, SHERRONE, ELIJAH INGRAM, CAMAY, OMIE, MATTY, ROSLYN, GATHERINE, GATHERLYN, AKBAR, NIAOMI, RONALD, FRED, WALI, RODNEY LEE, TIMMY, HENRIETTA, JAMIE, BRENDA, TERESA, ERIC, SHAWN, TRACEY, MELINDA, GEORGE COOPER, TAMIR GREEN, MIKE OSBORNE, G. RAMOS, BRO. DAOUD IBRAHEEM, W. SHEFFIELD, W. MORRIS, V. CIRINO, J. MOORE, MARSHALL, G. TYNER, M. LYNCH, KIRKLAND FAMILY, PASTER LUKE DAVIS OF GREATER HARVEST BAPTIST CHURCH, AND THOSE I HAVEN'T MENTION.

INTRODUCTION

This book is dedicated to my Wife
TRACY LIPSEY

I've been inspired by so many loving and caring people, without their unconditional support, this mind soothing book would not have come into existence, this work of art will take your perspective on life to another level, not down, but up. My book is written so simple a child will be able to comprehend. In all respect, I pray to "GOD" that something said in this book touches you in a helpful and God giving way, to strengthen your Life, Marriage, Family, Relationship or whatever dilemma that may arise in your journey and struggles through this awesome and wicked world. The only reason I wrote the book was to help someone. I'm so grateful and humble, thanking the heavenly father for giving me the gift to write and express my deepest thoughts, and concerns, enabling me to give it away, never expecting anything in return. I've learned some very valuable lessons in my life. I give God the praise for all things, good, bad, and not so good. I've come to realize that it is truly better to give any day than to receive. Last but definitely not least, life is very short, so live and enjoy it in a respectable and honest way.

TABLE OF CONTENT

ALWAYS GIVING

When you give your all, don't look for anything back
People don't think the same and that's a fact.

You can only give love and respect from the heart
Displaying how honest you are is where you start

Sometimes you're taken for granted
Before the seed is even planted

Judging plays the key role in a person eyes
Constantly looking at the what if and the whys

Giving of yourself to those who are in need
Will surely grant you serenity and good deeds

In the long run people will appreciate your sharing
Because deep inside it's all about caring

Understanding the very simple fact of giving
Puts you in touch with life and living

AMERICA WAR IN THE DESERT

America declared war the opposition is Iraq
Our troops are in the desert there's no turning back

It will be a bitter battle on the road to Baghdad
A war that will be relentless, bloody, heart felt and sad

The mission is to free the country and restore order
But first the soldiers have to control the Iraqi border

President has activated over 200,000 soldiers for war
Signs of another Vietnam knocking at America's door

This war will be far from a walk in the park
Facing the vicious sand storms will be rough and dark

We must pray for the POW's ask god to keep them safe
They are truly heroic for representing the United States

Some protester claim the war is simply over oil and power
Or could it be these terrorist planes crashing through the towers

The outcome of this war could be just a page in history
But for so many of us lost in doubt it's just a mystery

Whatever happened to Osama Bin Laden and Afghanistan?
He was America's most wanted man before Iraq and Saddam

Where could he be? We can not win this war until he's found
The search must be vigilant looking in every bunker underground

Destroy all Saddam's weapons of mass destruction it's a sin
Removing him from power will be a death match to the end

However this war should end, we must ask God for peace
And always remember that life started in the Middle East

To the soldiers in the front line stand tall, and stay alert
The objective of winning the war is showing your net worth

I hope and pray for our Troops a safe return back home
In the arms of their loving families whom they had to leave alone

BEING A MAN

As a child I dreamed of growing up and becoming a man
Taking on the responsibilities by doing the best I can

I know now that it's difficult being a man in this world
And it's a big difference between a little boy and a little girl

The man has to endure excessive, stress, defeat, and pain
Only through god's grace and mercy is man able to sustain

Man that is born of a woman is of few days
The book of job defines a man to be wicked in his ways

Every man wants to be a leader, dominate, conquer, and rule
Man's greatest asset is wisdom, his most powerful tool

I am a man full of confidence, dignity, most of all pride
Expressing my feelings as a man makes me strong inside

This message goes out to every man, black or white
The time has come for every man to respect the principals in his life

BEING YOURSELF

Most of us struggle with finding out who we are
Being yourself takes years of practice, just like driving a car

You must be patient in this growing process
Building your character, self esteem and happiness

Accepting yourself unconditionally, comes first not last
Giving one hundred percent of you will complete the task

As a child grows in different stages, body, and mind
Coming into adulthood our behavior changes with time

Along the way we learn faith in *God* which allows us to believe
Being yourself enables you to successfully achieve

There will come a time when you feel out of place
It's just your mental capacity craving for open space

So respect yourself by embracing spiritual peace within
Being yourself is the only way to play and win

BRICK CITY (NEWARK)

The Brick City defines the strength of a rock
Coming up you had to be hard to walk the block

I'm talking about Newark yeah'' my turf
The hardest City on the planet earth

Newark is a place filled with legends and winners
Some of the best prize fighters, teachers, and soul food dinners

They say New York is the City that never sleeps
Well Newark is the City where we play for keeps

When you come into the Brick City please beware
Watch your back because no one cares

The streets in the Brick City is no joke at all
Only the strong survive while the weak fall

The Brick City is a place that I love to hate
By the grace of God I survived so there's no debate

If you come from the Brick City you shine like a star
Your presence stands out no matter where you are

Living in the Brick City is hard but it's all good
It's the belly of the beast that's my ………… hood

I'm representing Brick City straight up and down
A message to fake jokers, cowards, and clowns

This poem goes out to Brick City, we stand alone
No other City can't compare, because we hold our own

DEAR GOD

D *ear* God I *just want to thank you for my life*
You have blessed me with three kids and a B *eautiful Wife*

I'm writing you this love letter with all my heart
Because you have been with me from the start

My dearest GOD *I pray to you each day and every night*
To lead me down the path to do what's right

You are the reason why I am still here today
The love I have inside for you is why I pray

There are so many things going on around me
Sometimes it's hard to accept what I see

I know that you hear my voice when I call your name
It's like going to the doctor when I'm in pain

You are my GOD, *my leader, strength, and confider*
Whenever I'm in need you are the provider

I want to say thank you once again
For being my GOD *and faithful friend*

DEATH

Life has a co–defendant and his name is death
He's the one that will take your last breath

Most of us don't understand why death seems so unkind
As we grow older it's engraved deep in our mind

Death has no particular date, time, or place
When your name is called, it means you've finished the race

Everyone will face death, there's no way to pass it by
People continue to ask god the number one question why

Death is a part of life's total concept and final address
You must experience it, to complete the process

No matter what type of life style you're living death is sure to come
It could be *a mother, father, sister, brother, daughter, or son*

We all should embrace death and its great impact
The mental and spiritual powers of a godly act

DERAILED

When two people can't see eye to eye
It could be time for them to say good-bye

Sometimes it's hard to walk away from love
The only cure is prayer to God up above

Over a period of time the pain and memory fade
Those are the choices in life that you both made

The pointing of fingers on who should take the blame
It's a part of what goes down in the relationship game

Questions come up about what went wrong
And why two loving and caring people just couldn't get along

Hearts are broken and no one seems to care
Leaving someone can be so sad and unfair

You ask yourself was it worth the time
On some days the sun didn't shine

Now that it's over you take a look back
Only to find out that love just simply fell off track

DRUG ADDICTION

Drug Addiction is lonely, painful, sad, and unfair
When you're addicted to drugs you're going no where

Using drugs always starts out like its big fun
Then all hell breaks loose like a baby holding a loaded gun

Drugs will destroy whoever gets in its path
No one uses drugs successfully you do the math

There are over a million people addicted to drugs today
Some want to get off but don't know the right way

The days and nights have no meaning they just pass by
Using drugs are truly the world's greatest lie

If you think using drugs is cool I suggest you think twice
The repercussions in the end are never kind or nice

I share this poem about drug addiction and I hope that it's heard
Because it's a genocide of all cultures in every sense of the word

There will come a time when the drugs take total control
Decreasing your life span shutting down the body and soul

Everyday someone passes away from the drug abuse
We need to find a solution to stop this killer on the loose

Families are suffering our children confused they don't understand
The wickedness of drugs have conquered in full command

Drugs are an excuse for those who tend to be weak
People who are not willing to stand on their own two feet

If you're using drugs and you don't know the real reason why
Just tell yourself I want to live before I die

EAT OR BEATEN
FIGHT OR BE BEATEN

They said I would never succeed and always fail
That my life was cursed my destination was hell

There was no hope for me only a matter of time
Before the forces of wickedness destroyed my mind

I refused to take the degradation on the chin
Instead I made a vow to fight to the very end

Inside my heart I knew God would be there for me
God has guided me through many storms unconditionally

All my life I've been judged to do wrong not right
Only to prove that I am the sun which represent light

No matter what's said I will do my very best
I will follow in Jesus' name and nothing less

FEELING GOOD

Feel good about who you are
Everybody can't be a star

Thank God for another day
Tomorrow has to come some how some way

So be happy, joyous, and free
Think about people who you can't see

Your heart should be filled with love
A gift sent from the God above

Take care of your body and mind
Because the two are one of a kind

You should be grateful that you are here
Today, tomorrow and maybe next year

Embrace yourself, because you deserve the best
Pursue all of your dreams and nothing less

It's so important to know how you truly feel
Feeling good about yourself by keeping it real

FIREFIGHTERS

Firefighters are truly the best at what they do
Saving lives and putting out fires just to name a few

Their greatest task was demonstrated at ground zero
Proved to be Americas true and dedicated heroes

Every hat should come off for the firefighters of 9/11
Firefighters went down but they all were sent to heaven

God opened up the golden gates, calling each one
Letting them know what a great job they had done

Every man, woman and child must bow their head and pray
Giving thanks to the firefighters on that tragic day

Firefighters have been around for many years
Placing their lives on the line through blood sweat and tears

They are definitely a class act without a doubt
Whenever there is a fire, sirens you hear engine numbers in route

FRIENDS

I thought that we were friends and would always be
All of a sudden you started to change on me

Friends are to honor, respect, and love one another
A relationship equal to a sister and a brother

When we first met I knew from the start
You and I as friends would never part

What happened to the friendship we once had
Why did it have to end so bitter and sad

The memories still linger forever in my mind
Because as friends we became one of a kind

If I had one wish that could come true
It would be to bring back the friend I had in you

They say that a friend is what everybody need
Friends come and grow just like planting a seed

FROM THE HEART

The time has come for me to say what I feel
My insides are hurting and the pain is unreal

Each breath I take seems like my last
I ask God to forgive me for the things of my past

There are things that I want to say that won't come out
It makes me wonder why there is so much doubt

Saying what's in my heart can be a difficult task
Maybe that's why for years I've worn a mask

I'm now learning how to speak what's on my mind
Because my heart is pure and one of a kind

My life is built on trust, honesty, and respect
Without those three main ingredients my feelings are not correct

On a deeper level I must always speak the truth
The look in my eyes will be my only proof

Everyone has to learn how to express what's inside
Letting it out will strengthen your heart and pride

GETTING THROUGH THE STORM

There are some days that you would rather forget all about, never realizing that in life those days are simply storms that you must encounter to get to the other side. There will be some very bitter storms, calm storms, heavy storms, long storms, in regards to the types of storms we face as human beings, it's not one we can't get through. The number one antidote consists of daily prayer and faith in god, ask god for support and guidance. Without storms or problems, which have the same effect, life would be simple, living without going through storms is impossible, we must face storms to appreciate the blessings that god has in store for us. In the world today it is very difficult to relax, because you never know the exact day and time that your storm will come, in your journey through life prepare yourself to be strong, staying alert and focused through gods grace and mercy the storms will pass you by.

GIVING UP

This message is about losing focus and giving up, no matter what. There will come a time in your life when you are really feeling down about yourself, thinking that everything that can go wrong has turned out just that way, these moments come when you least expect. Giving up is so simple, it doesn't take any deep thinking, just impulsive reaction. Giving up on yourself will definitely lead you on a path of self destruction, pity, fear, and low self esteem. Giving up on opportunities that you are worthy of means you didn't give your all. Giving up defines ones mental weakness, unwilling to fight or stand up for what you believe in. When you give up, it means you didn't try hard enough, if you don't have faith you will always give up. Before you entertain the thought about giving up, I suggest you think about the repercussions.

GROWING UP

There comes a time in your life when you have to grow up, taking on responsibilities that you will embark upon in your journey through this troubled world. We all must travel the path of righteousness and wickedness there's no escape clause, shortcuts, or loopholes, it's only one way. In order to be successful in life your faith has to out weigh your feelings, because in all actuality your growth is based solely on having faith in god. We must stand up and compete at every level, accepting defeat and disappointments as they arise, without those two common denominators you have no room to grow up, as a baby in your mothers womb the growing process begins, once you exit the womb you learn the basic rule's to growing up, the difference between what's hot, what's good and bad, the list goes on. Growing in childhood is like an adventure, growing up in adulthood is when reality sets in and it becomes more of a challenge.

HISTORY

People that live for a long time and get up in age
Should be honored with respect because they set the stage

Their longevity defines, experience, strength, and hope
Sharing their wisdom, visions and even funny jokes

We must always remember to acknowledge their position
It teaches us how to focus on our mission

Without their existence, and belief in God's grace
Life would simply be a winless race

Give them a holiday on the calendar each new year
Let's celebrate their contributions for being here

It's truly a blessing to stand here on this day
And pay homage long over due to the silver and gray

Although you're called seniors who are truly young at heart
God has definitely created a beautiful work of art

This poem goes out to those who are older than me
Thank you for passing down your lessons on history

The word humble is very meaningful and profound
To embrace it you have to be spiritually sound

In order to find peace we must become humble
Your life without it will definitely crumble

It's not easy and everyone has to stumble
That's the only way we learn how to become humble

To be loyal, humble, generous and kind
Pray to god for the purest heart and an open mind

Try your best to stay humble in this world today
Take time to meditate is truly the only way

IF GOD WENT ON STRIKE TODAY

If *GOD* went on strike today
Tomorrow would quickly fade away

You would be lost, confused, and afraid
Just like working and not getting paid

Imagine living in darkness without light
Unable to determine the day from night

If *GOD* went on strike today
Life wouldn't be worth living anyway

There would be no clouds, moon, or sun up in the sky
The time would stop and everything on earth would die

If *GOD* went on strike today what would you do
Hope and pray that you make it through

The world would be without a leader and provider
Our true source of strength and only confider

We would have to give back all material things
Cars, homes, clothes, precious pearls and diamond rings

Life would be a nightmare and not a sweet dream
The devil would praise *GOD* by all means

If *GOD* went on strike today we couldn't live
Because he take life and also life he gives

Those of us who suffer from the disease of addiction
Defines an example of *God* going on strike affliction

If *God* went on strike today
There would be nothing anybody could say

Everything you thought was yours is taken
Your life and loved ones all forsaken

There would be no need to complain or cry
Or even ask *God* why

We would all suffer the pain and life would end
If *God* went on strike today it would be a sin

I WANT TO LIVE

I want to live to be eighty or more
I want to live like never before

I want to live because I'm happy today
I want to live to see the blessings come my way

I want to live today and think about tomorrow
I want to live through the pain and sorrow

I want to live in a state of peace of mind
I want to live because life is so divine

I want to live and travel from coast to coast
I want to live my life to the utter most

I want to live each day in a positive mode
I want to live to be one hundred years old

I want to live is my mission on this earth
I want to live that's why my mother gave birth

I want to live to be a husband to my wife
I want to live because I truly respect life

I want to live before the day I die
I want to live forever and it's a reason why

I want to live should be everyone's creed
I want to live is how we plant the seed

JUDGING WRONG AND RIGHT

When you think something is wrong it could be right
Figuring out the two could cause a sleepless night

It is very important that you confide in god with your heart
Because as human beings, wrong and right can be confusing at
the start

Understanding wrong and right stems from your deepest thoughts
It's no guarantee and it can't be sold or bought

You must be honest and sincere about wrong and right
God created heaven, earth, darkness, and light

I think it's wrong to make something right look bad
Feelings get hurt and the whole situation becomes sad

Wrong and right, true and false, yes and no, love and hate
Are words we continue to struggle with and debate?

As you travel through life these eight words you will face
Make sure that you put them in the proper place

Judging someone based on wrong and right I don't think it's fair
You should take time to look into their heart if you really care

KEEP YOUR HEAD UP

Keep your head up there's no need to look down
People who are not focused wear the frown

Looking up allows you to see what's in front and back
And the only way to avoid any negative contact

You praise god by looking up at the sky
Blessings come down by holding your head up high

I will keep my head up no matter what it takes
Through the sunshine, bitter storms and heartaches

By holding your head up you're able to see another day
Giving yourself the opportunity that's bound to come
your way

Just by holding your head up builds self esteem
You can see the development of all your hopes and dreams

LEADERS

I am a leader the one that knows the right way
You can follow me and I'll show you how to play

A true leader will take you where you need to go
He's prepared and conditioned from head to toe

Leaders come and go but they will always be around
New leaders replace the old just like the lost and found

In order to be a leader you must be god sent
Leaders are born with visions, goals, and commitments

Loving and caring defines what a leader really means
Every good leader has a successful story and a dream

Sometimes their mission can seem impossible to reach
Pursuing goals and commitments is what real leaders teach

Leaders of our past were strong honorable and great
That's why the leader's today must be on time, never late

We need leaders to direct, suggest and dictate the next move
Every leader has a plan and their own special set of rules

Leaders work twenty four hours in a day and get very little sleep
Their job consist of guiding the nation while strengthening the weak

When you encounter a leader you'll know who they are
All leaders possess a glow that shines just like a star

Leaders are at the top of the game always doing their best
Playing with dedication, determination and finesse

LIFE FROM MY POINT OF VIEW

Life is full of trouble, short and unfair
Sometimes I wonder does God really care

There are people in my life who I love very much
My heart yearn everyday for their tender touch

I continue to play by the rules of the game
Looking for a way to win without feeling shame

It seems like you can't do anything right
Making you uncomfortable getting to sleep at night

Life brings about different problems and pain
If you are not strong it can drive you insane

Human beings go through some difficult times
Life can be a struggle and the sun don't always shine

We must understand that life comes with a price
Whether you're good or bad you don't live twice

Whenever you fail a test in life take it on the chin
Remember that it's more ways than one to win

The life you live will be your own
Giving your all can set the tone

Understanding that the road you travel will be rough
Life in general will forever be tough

The time will come when things go wrong
Some are weak and some are strong

Life can make you feel extremely low
Try your best to stay focused and finish the show

LIFE IS PRECIOUS

Sometimes in our travels we take life for granted
Showing no appreciation for the seed that has been planted

Looking at everything from a negative perspective
Instead of keeping our focus on the main objective

You must prepare for the battle that waits down the road
As a child growing up this story was often told

Remember that you are only passing through
Respect yourself so that God should grant you

The only way to get ahead and reach the top
You have to play a solid game, fast pace and non- stop

Life is precious no matter how you feel
So embrace it each day by simply keeping it real

LIFE
IS
SHORT

No matter how hard life gets
You must keep fighting and never quit

We all have to endure the ups and downs
It's a part of being lost and found

When you give your all in a game
Win, lose or draw there's no need to feel shame

The time will come for you to compete
Step up to the plate and feel the heat

Every soul has that burning desire
GOD grants us blessings to reach even higher

LOOKING INTO THE MIRROR

Looking into the mirror and what do I see
The reflection of a person who looks like me

When I speak to him/ her the response is the same
The mirror tells a story of fortune, fame, and even shame

My image can be seen in every mirror of the world
It has the glow of a diamond, ruby, and a precious pearl

Take time to look into the mirror each day
Thank god that you can see another way

I can see myself through a magnifying glass
Growing in stages as time continues to pass

Who I am is what I see on the other side
When looking into the mirror there's nothing to hide

The mirror tells the truth about who you are
Allowing you to reach no matter how far

To see yourself in the mirror just take a look
Stare with deep concentration like reading a book

Everyone has to look into the mirror at a point in time
To understand the power of the mirror is so sublime

As you look into the mirror you start to dream
Your eyes have a vision that's gifted and supreme

Losing a Love One

Losing a precious loved one is the most difficult time in our life. The passing of a loved has to be dealt with unconditionally, it is a very bitter pill to swallow. The lost of a loved one can destroy your life; it can weaken you to a point of sickness. Losing a loved one will definitely bring us to our knees. Asking so many questions, but until we get involved in the word of god spiritually, most of us will never understand the true essence of losing love ones. When we embrace god with our heart our understanding will come over a period of time. Even then accepting the lost of a love one will be devastating. It will take many years before you honestly find a way to accept and surrender to the fact that losing a loved one is truly a godly act. If you ask someone this question, when you part this life where do we expect to go and their response is heaven, there's no other place that they will mention. Heaven to me is the after life, high above the clouds in the sky, it surpasses the moon, sun, and the stars. Heaven is where we go when our time on this earth is over.

LOVE

Love can be expressed in so many ways; the main ingredient comes from deep within your heart and soul. Love is a very powerful and profound word given only from God and spread all across the entire Universe. Love can make you do some very wonderful things; it can also be baffling and deceiving. When we allow ourselves to embrace the true meaning of love, life becomes worth living, you begin to see everything around you in a different perspective. Love has its changes, bitter and sweet, hot and cold, right or wrong. To know love you must developed an honest and sincere understanding of what it really feels like to be loved. In order to love someone, you must first demonstrate the love you have for god and yourself, because that is the foundation. The root of love, in the scriptures it states that god so loved the world that he gave his only be gotten son. Love can heal a broken heart. It can bring peace to mankind; it can build a happy home. The list of love goes on, and on it has no limitations on how deep love goes.

maintaining my square

Maintaining my square by staying on my feet
Accepting the challenge always willing to compete

The main ingredient consist of having faith in you
Making sure your square stays firm is not hard to do

You must probe for weak areas around your square
It could cause a great deal of harm so beware

There's only one square you can claim
Your responsibility is to honor, respect, and maintain

My number one concern is keeping my square with me
Giving god praise for his grace and mercy

MAINTAINING YOUR FOCUS

There are times when I feel so alone
My state of mind seems far from home

I try to stay humble, honest, and strong
Praising god for guiding me along

When I think about things in the past
It makes me wonder how long will I last

Every year that passes by I'm getting older
They say that beauty is in the eyes of the beholder

The time is now for me to take a stand
Accepting my responsibilities and being who I am

New feelings come and go each day
Don't take them personal it's just that way

Today you must pray for tomorrow to come
Because feelings are real within everyone

We must express what's deep inside
It helps build your character and pride

Your focus will determine which route you take
Allowing you to keep it real and not fake

Just remember to focus on the body and mind
Peace and love you will always find

MONEY

The one thing that everyone strives for is called money
It's an essential need in this land of milk and honey

With money you can travel the world and even rule
Money pays for medical, meals, and school

There are several ways to earn money today
By working steady and diligent is the best way

Money will help you get through the hard times
Some people receive money by way of violent crimes

We all want money to buy nice material things
Only God grants us money and the joy it brings

MOTHER

A mother is a diamond, pearl and a precious jewel
She's the only one that will understand, dominate, and rule

When no one else would listen to your cry
A mother would do her best to help you get by

A mother is always there when you need her the most
Never complaining why you've gone from pillar to post

My mother will forever be placed in a class of her own
She will always stand up on the highest throne

A mother dictates the process and the pace
Giving you the confidence in winning the race

A mother is God's gift to every mans hopes and dreams
That's why he is able to go to great lengths and extremes

A mother is truly the head of the flock
Making sure the meals are served around the clock

A mother is always there when something goes wrong
She's the one that inspires you and tells you to be strong

A mother teaches you God's mercy and his grace
Telling you stories about how heaven is such a special place

A mother is the foundation on which we have learned to live
A mother's main goal is to raise her children to be positive

MOTHER'S DAY

When mother's day comes along it's always a special time
We must honor all mothers for their strength is so divine

If it wasn't for mother's we would not exist on earth
Thank God for creating mothers to give birth

Every mother, young and old should celebrate on this day
Your teachings of love, respect, and courage have paved the way

Mother's have weathered many storms, man could never endure
God created mother's to be loving, honest, warm, and pure

Mothers are the true essence of God's creation in life
Their powerful gift to give birth and own the title of wife

I extend mothers day greetings to the mothers that are not here
Because inside our hearts their love will forever be near

Mother's should be commemorated and cherished to the end
Anything less would be considered a cardinal sin

Let's take mother's day to another level, give them props
Everyday should be mother's day; they are the head of the crops

This poem goes out to all the mothers, you know who you are
Wishing you the happiest mother's day while shining like a star

MY ADORABLE WIFE

I can truly say that god blessed me with a lovely wife
It has been revealed, that's why she's so important in my life

We have weathered some very bitter storms
Understanding god's will we were definitely informed

If you looked up wife in the dictionary her picture would show
My wife warms my heart with her special glow

I really do my very best to let her know I care
The love I have for her is all that I share

We have been together for over twenty years
We've shared joy, pain, laughter, and tears

She's without a doubt my only precious jewel
She's so sweet, fair and kind always plays by the rules

My wife has given me something worth more than gold
Three beautiful children whom I love to hold

When I speak about my wife and what she means to me
I honestly thank the lord above for her generosity

MY BATTLES

I've been through some hard times I can't forget
Coming up I had to fight, steal, cheat, and sweat

I remember those nights without lights or heat
A lot of days I had to go to bed with nothing to eat

My mother worked as a house cleaner to earn money
We lived very poor in this land they call milk and honey

My childhood consisted of survival, faith, and sacrifice
I learned early on how to read, write, and think twice

I was introduced to god at a very early age
Through my mother's spiritual connection she set the stage

Everyday I learned something important and new
It was those lessons of tough love that guided me through

Today I can stand here and tell the world about me
I don't have to feel ashamed of how it used to be

I am proud of myself; I've come such a long way
I continue to fight the battle of growing day by day

My father instilled in me the definition of being a man
He taught me to be strong, confident and now I understand

I will teach my children how to face their battles and win
Encourage them to challenge life to the end

MY DAUGHTER'S

My daughter's are precious they're my little pearls
They are truly daddy's most favorite girls

Their hearts are warm, pure, and sincere
I have two daughters that I love so dear

When I call on one the other comes too
This poem is for Manisa and Samira daddy loves you

The oldest is nineteen the youngest is eight
I believe in my heart they are angels and my soul mates

The love they have for me you can't buy
That's why I will love my daughter's until I die

MY FATHER

My father taught me how to be a man
He didn't do it by raising his hand

His wisdom, knowledge, and pure heart
Played the most important part

He always had positive words to say
Teaching me how to do things the *man* way

My father gave me his very best
Enabling me to pass the man's test

I will honor my father until the day I die
Because he was the best father in my eyes

My father was loving, caring and shared his mind
Helping those in need he was one of a kind

He was my father my brother and friend
My love for him stays deep within

He was my father, I was his only son
Together we will be forever as one

MY FIVE SISTERS'

I have five sisters whom I love very much
They all are loving, caring and possess a tender touch

My sisters and I share a special bond
Whenever I call on them they all respond

I love my sisters all the same
Each one of them has a special name

Nancy, Sue, Eileen, Baba, and Bunny
When God created them it was milk and honey

My sister's each hold the title of mother
All have something special in common their only brother

My sisters will forever be inside my heart
As their only brother we will never part

I truly and sincerely thank God for these five ladies
There are no ifs, ands, buts, or maybes

MY GRANDMOTHER

My grandmother is the reason why I'm here today
I thank God for her each time I kneel and pray

Growing up as kids we called her mama Joan
She will always be in a class of her own

Her encouraging words of wisdom keep me mentally strong
Motivates me in everyway to do right not wrong

My grandmother is truly, kind, charming, and sincere
I am forever grateful to have my grandmother here

The love I have for her lives deep inside of me
She's the root, head of the flock and my history

It's a blessing to write this poem on her behalf
The matriarch was born in 1915 you do the math

Although I don't see her everyday I do use the phone
Just to hear her voice and that youthful tone

This poem goes out to my grandmother whom I adore
Thank you for being my grandmother and much, much more

MY LIFE

My life is very special and dear to me
I'm so happy, proud, joyous, and free

I thank the almighty God for his grace
Giving me the strength to keep up the pace

Physically and mentally I feel young at heart
Staying in shape plays the biggest part

Taking care of myself by doing what's right
Facing my fears each day and night

Love and respect defines what I'm all about
That's why I love me without any doubts

Living my life has its shares of ups and downs
Self motivation keeps my feet on solid ground

There are times when I'm in deep pain
Wondering how long will I be able to sustain

Telling myself that I'm on the right track
Just continue to go forward and don't turn back

At the young tender age of forty one
I am truly blessed my life has just begun

Living my life is truly a blessing
Enabling me to grow without too much stressing

Accepting my life with good and bad
Keeping it real about the happy and sad

MY MOTHER IN – LAW

My dear mother in-law has a special place in my heart
The love she showed me was truly a work of art

I will miss her everyday for the rest of my life
Thanking her for giving birth to my adorable wife

My mother in-law will always be very dear to me
The love I have for her was so real and easy to see

I was her only son in- law and proud as can be
She's in a special place away from the pain and misery

My mother in-law Mrs. Shirley Purnell
Her kind heart and charming ways could cast a spell

She had a beautiful smile and a very soft touch
When I first met her I knew I would love her just that much

MY NUMBER ONE

My number one wish in life, is to be with only you
These words that I share are honest, sincere, and true

You are the glass of water that quenches my thirst
I place you in a class of your own, always first

There's not a day that goes by, without you on my mind
The power of your love, so sweet, pure, and divine

I thank my god everyday, for lending you to me
Our love goes deeper, than the great red sea

We can travel and have fun even take long walks
Cuddle up in bed and share our deepest thoughts

So if you have any doubts on how much I really care
Just look over your shoulder and I'll be right there

All I need is you to complete this book of life
I dedicate this poem to my sweet and lovely wife

MY SON

I will teach him how to be a man
Share my knowledge and extend my hand

Give him all my love, strength, and advice
Instill in him to think not once but twice

Correcting him whenever he does wrong
Define the true meaning of being strong

I am his father, mentor, role model, and friend
Our bond is forever and deep within

Spending time with him makes me feel good
Watching him grow into the stage of manhood

He is my partner, my hero, my twin, my son
I thank God for blessing me with just one

MY WRITING

My **Writing** skills are meant to be heard
Sharing true feelings and my honest word

The message I send may reach only a few
I hope and pray that it's one of you

My writing takes me on an everlasting ride
Enabling me to show what's really deep inside

What I write about is based on godly acts
My awareness on the world and facts

Taking it to another level describes my writing
Giving my all to the reader makes it more exciting

Feel my words with your total open mind
Because this kind of writing is one of a kind

God has blessed me with the gift to write
I will treasure it for the rest of my life

NEVER GIVE UP

There will come a time in your life when everything seems to go wrong. Despite how bad things may get never give up. These cycles will arise unexpectedly, just be willing to stand up and move on. If you believe in yourself and you're spiritually sound there's no way you'll give up. Never give up should be your motivating factor, never give up on your hopes and dreams. Never give up on things that seem out of reach, it simply means that it's reachable. Never give up on your daily prayer because that is your lethal weapon and it will never betray you. You should never give up, never give up.

NUMBER ONE

No matter what you think of me, it's okay
I just ask God to forgive me when I pray

People will judge me even when I die
There's no need for me to worry or wonder why

My mission today is to take care of me
Letting go of my past and how it used to be

Giving myself a chance is what I really need
Staying positive in mind while planting my seed

Trying to please everybody all the time
Placing myself at the end of the line

Those days are over there's no coming back
It's my time to shine and that's a fact

I have given my all by extending my hand
Helping those in need has made me a better man

PARENTAL GUIDANCE

*O*ur children are not given a fair chance. Most of the parents are single parents, some are on drugs, and alcohol. In majority of cases, the fathers are incarcerated or just too selfish to own up to being a father. I think that it's a travesty for our kids. They deserve to be treated with pure love and affection, taught right from wrong. We as parents suppose to make sure that our children are on the right path as far as god, education, discipline, and self respect. Teaching them how to build up their self esteem, instill in your children that they can achieve whatever the mind conceives. Allow them to express themselves in difficult situations. The parents are responsible for guiding their children in a positive direction. To a certain degree we have to be held accountable for our children's actions, because it all starts at home. If the parents don't step up to the plate and become mother's and father's, our beautiful little angels, given to us from the heavenly father are going to fall by the way side.

PEACE INSTEAD OF WAR

America has its vision and mind on going to war
When the crime and murder rate here continues to soar

What will it prove to wipe out a country like Iraq
Or could it be to even the score on the WTC attack

I think the president should reconsider this mission
Before putting this country in an awkward position

There's a better solution than fighting and killing
This world needs peace, prayer, and God's healing

War has never solved the problem, it just made it worse
We're living the times of wickedness with a curse

I'm calling on all nations for united we stand
Let's drop the weapons of destruction, and join hands

Our children are growing at a rapid pace
They deserve a fair chance in life's awesome race

PEOPLE, PLACES, AND THINGS

We live in a world filled with people, places, and things
With seasons of summer, winter, fall and spring

There are so many places you can travel today
North, south, east, and west, round trip or one way

God created this world and seasons so we could live
Giving us things to do on our journey that's positive

The seasons change as the months go by
You can detect one from the other just by looking at the sky

Winter is cold, summer is hot, spring is warm, and fall is cool
The four seasons each have their own set of rules

People in this world are the heart and mind
They generate action, excitement and dictate time

PRAYER

*P*rayer and meditation can be such a relaxing and mind soothing medicine. Prayer allows you to connect with your spiritual and inner feelings. Prayer brings you in contact with God. As individuals we will find peace and mind. Prayer is practiced daily, everyday. Prayer equals faith; prayer will solve the most difficult problems that life has to offer. Prayer builds your self esteem, confidence, tolerance, and your belief system. Prayer heals the mind, body, and soul. Prayer and faith can take you places you've always dreamed of going. Prayer has to be the start of your day and the middle of your day and the ending. We must pray for all things created by God. Prayer allows you to embrace life in every aspect, prayer guides you through all the difficult situations that you may encounter, continue to use prayer, it's your only hope.

PRISON

Prison is a place where your, life disappears
Locked in a keyless cell for many years

Stripped of your freedom and civil rights
Everyday in prison is a sleepless night

You are sentenced by a judge and confined
Based on the jury, you committed the crime

There are so many wasted lives in prison today
Their hopes and dreams continue to fade away

The prisons are filled with young and old
Each one has a story, that's bitter and cold

Life inside prison can be excruciating pain
Having true faith in god will help you sustain

This poem goes out to those that are in prison
Set goals today, for tomorrow will come your vision

PROBLEMS

In and throughout life you will have to endure problems time after time, there are no limitations. As human beings we must adjust our mental capacity to be able to handle the difficult situations that are bound to pass our way. First and foremost you must accept Jesus our lord and savior in your life, he's our only hope. Without him we are like birds with no wings, you must believe in yourself in order to grow and be serene. That manifest comes with our growth mechanism. Problems are strictly apart of our living. They come at the most awkward times and it can sometimes be overwhelming.

QUITTERS

Quitters in the game of life never win their race
They don't have the endurance to keep up the pace

Always giving up before ever getting started
Looking at everything they do half hearted

Quitters don't believe that there is a way
Unwilling to face the fact that they must pay

Quitters will do whatever it takes to lose
Going to great lengths and breaking all the rules

Quitter's main goal is to stay at the end of the line
Lost, confused, out of sight and out of mind

Quitters are the people that don't like to play
Afraid of the outcome at the end of the day

Quitters are lonely, close minded, scared, and shy
That's the definition of a quitter in a winner's eye

RACISM

I can't wait for the day that racism will end
For over three hundred years it has been a painful sin

The attitude and behavior of people must change
Although to the majority it will always be the same

I think it is ignorant and inhumane to practice hate
In God's eyes we are all equal there's no debate

Racism was created by a particular cultural race
To gain superiority by the mere look on your face

Our children are totally unaware of racism's great impact
We must teach them its true meaning and known facts

It doesn't matter what complexion you have at birth
The content of your character will determine your net worth

All human being's should be proud of who they are
Cause whether you're black or white you're still a potential star

The time has come to accept each other with a warm embrace
Living in this world today we are all running the same race

Racism is a disease, designed to destroy and divide
By conquering a mass of people taking away their pride

There are so many different *shades* of people, *dark* and *light*
That might be separate but yet equal just like day and night

So before you judge someone by the *color* of his or her skin
Take a good look it's not on the outside but deep within

RAISING THE BAR

At a certain stage you must raise the bar
If you fail to do so it can leave a scar

This is an important step we can't ignore
It's the elevator going to the next floor

Our greatest challenge is facing the fear to rise
Having true faith in God will be your only guide

By raising the bar determines your status and growth
In a court of law it's a crime to lie under oath

There's always room to improve so raise the bar
Why settle for the moon when you can be a star

REALITY

Waking up to reality is not always a sweet dream
We have to face reality by all means

Reality enables you to accept life on its own terms
Dealing with reality is one of our greatest concerns

Reality can cost you heart ache, pain, and fear
There's no way to avoid reality it will always be here

Reality has a special method of showing us truth
Everyone will embrace reality, it's the living proof

When reality is planted in your body and mind
You are qualified to stand in the reality line

Reality is defined by God's mercy and grace
We have to understand that reality is the real race

SMILE

There's nothing more healing than a warm smile
Whether given or receiving it's always worth while

A smile takes away the bitter frown on a face
Praising God will keep that bright smile in place

When you smile, it means everything is all right
Your spirit is filled with happiness each day and night

On the contrary, some of us smile to cover up pain
That's a smile we find hard to sustain

Smile and the sun will shine your way
Or just watch the children as they run and play

If you don't smile then something is wrong
Maybe you're in a place where you don't belong

SOME PEOPLE IN THIS WORLD

In this world there are some people who really don't care
They'll take your kindness for granted and that's unfair

Showing how ungrateful in every way they can
Some people can be very difficult to understand

When you share your heart don't expect theirs in return
Some people will disappoint you by showing no concern

When you are loving, honest, kind, and sincere
Some people take your humble ways in total fear

It's very important to be careful in this world today
Some people will hurt and harm you in every way

Being to friendly can cause a great deal of pain
Some people in this world will always live in vain

There is no unity, loyalty, or simply respect
Some people just don't understand life's total concept

If this world is to become a better place
Some people need to realize this is the earth not space

STRUGGLES

The struggles are coming that we must face
There's always a struggle in each competitive race

It's no easy route or shortcut along the way
"God" will guide you through your struggles everyday

Struggles will be large, medium, and small
You have to accept each struggle, one in all

When things appear alright, a struggle, is always near
You can't avoid a struggle, there's nothing to fear

We struggle only to be compensated in the end
Success will not exist without a struggle, every now and then

Struggles teach you how to live, love, appreciate, and survive
Overcoming our struggles enables us to enjoy life's awesome
ride

Remember your struggles and how they made you feel
Behind every struggle there's a lesson and blessing so real

SUCCESS

Each individual should have the desire to win
By doing their best from beginning to end

Success comes to those who work hard
Anyone can achieve that success card

Give yourself a chance and you will see
Success doesn't cost anything its really free

Self confidence is all it takes to play
If you stay focused success will come your way

You should feel positive about being a success
And never settle for anything lower or less

Remember, success is right next door to you
Whenever you want it, just reaching out will do

TAKING A WALK WITH PRIDE

As I walked down the block, people began to stare
My state of mind was positive, so I didn't care

They looked me up and down, whispering words
I figured it was simply just for the birds

So I kept moving, at a smooth and steady pace
The sounds I heard didn't have a matching face

Whenever I'm in the public eye, business, or pleasure
I know that I'm noticed and even measured

It's a good feeling to stand out in the crowd
Showing that you're egotistical, confident and proud

THE AFTERMATH OF 9 - 11- 01

*T*he tears in many eyes will continue to drop
It was September 11, the day when time stopped

We must remember forever in our hearts
So many lives lost, happy families torn apart

Some of us ask God how this could be
Why is the world filled with such evil and envy?

These two countries involved in this terror attack
Whom America claims were Afghanistan and Iraq

They'll have to answer for America's suffering and pain
Terrorism is truly an act of ignorance and totally insane

The time has come for America to take a stand
Seek out justice against Bin Laden and Saddam

They are number one on the most wanted list
Let's hope and pray they're found, *charged,* and *punished*

If the U.S. let's this pass these acts of terror will go on for years
This mighty nation shall rise up and face our fears

My prayers go out to the families of the victims of nine eleven
I truly believe each one have successfully made it to heaven

THE BROTHERS TODAY

WHAT'S WRONG WITH THE BROTHERS TODAY?

Gang banging, robbing, and killing
Portraying the role of a cold blooded villain

The brothers today have taken a turn for the worst
I think this generation of brothers has been cursed

The prison population is predominately filled with brothers
They leave home and abandoned their mothers

Our brothers are confused, lost and out of control
Their definition of life consist of a deep black hole

There are so many brothers losing in the game of life
Leaving behind son's, daughter's and the precious wife

Bullets continue cutting down brother's everyday
Sometimes I wonder why it has to be this way

Brothers need to wake up and show some respect
Remember the million man march when brothers we're in check

The time is now for brothers to take a stand
Stop recording negative music to please the other man

The brothers today must open their hearts and mind
By reading the scriptures of God the brother's will find

I'm calling on all brothers North, South, East, and West
Let's come together in peace, love and happiness

Everyday that the brothers live, it is truly a blessing
It's the brother's duty to learn that important lesson

What's going on with the brothers doesn't make any sense
Brothers killing brothers is not even a coincidence

If these issues with the brothers continue to take place
Our future brothers to come will lose the race

This message goes out to the brothers please hear my cries
I hope that one day my brothers open up their eyes

THE CREATOR

When you call on me, I'm always right there
If you listen close, you can hear my voice in the air

I control, complete, compare, and dictate on and off
Focus your attention; you'll feel my spirit, my touch, so soft

Although you can't see me with the naked eye
You can communicate with me, by holding your head up high

Respecting my powers, I know can be hard to do
You could never become me because I created you

I have over a thousand names, and will answer to them all
I'm the one that catches you, when you stumble or fall

So many individuals have tried to impersonate me
Only to fail the test of finding out my true mystery

I am Alpha and Omega the creator of heaven and earth
On the Day of Judgment I will determine your net worth

THE DAYS

Yesterday told tomorrow to call today, today told tomorrow I'll be right there, when yesterday went away, today became all alone, and yesterday became just another day. Today the sun was shining, yesterday it rained, tomorrow the world will turn and begin a new today. The circle of yesterday, tomorrow, and today can create, dictate, what, when, where, and who. If it wasn't for yesterday, tomorrow could never exist, today would have no purpose or meaning. Yesterday said good-bye because tomorrow is on the way, but when today came, yesterday and tomorrow will simply fade away.

"THAT'S DEEP"

THE DEFINITION OF LIFE

I've always wanted to live good and do well
My destination in life, I chose heaven over hell

When growing up, all I did was wish and dream
Of becoming a super star on a big movie screen

Where I come from, you had to step up to the plate
It was like playing baseball, three strikes, not eight

In order for me to take it to the next page
My whole life had to change, not just my age

I thank God every day for keeping me alive
It's only through his grace and mercy, I continue to survive

Looking over my life and where I'm at today
If I had a second life, I would live it the same way

You are only as good as you think you are
Reaching your goals is similar to driving a car

Following my heart has brought me tons of success
By refusing to lose, I have past life's ultimate test

To be a success you have to struggle every now and then
That's the definition of life and the only way to win

THE FINAL DEBATE

It will come a time for the final debate
Your thoughts are important so don't discriminate

The final debate will keep us safe and sound
We must remember that life is extremely profound

Making our decisions based on positive facts
The final debate is not a contract

We have gone through some very rough times
This is the final debate where we draw the line

Can we work out a final debate, I hope you agree
God made all this possible it's so plain to see

The final debate will depend on what we feel
Over twenty years of marriage with a golden seal

We come thus far by love and faith
There's no ending just simply the final debate

Looking back in time, no particular place or state
Shows our level of growth and the final debate

I wouldn't change anything and it's never too late
What we need the most is the final debate

THE GHETTO

A place that's filled with sorrow, sadness, and pain
Where dreams of success go down the drain

The ghetto is truly the belly of the beast
Everywhere you go there's a ghetto, North, West, South,
or East

Poverty and crime are at the top of the list
If you live in the ghetto your census count doesn't exist

Chances of becoming a star in the ghetto are slim to none
Our kids education consist of violence, drugs and the
smoking gun

The ghetto will forever be a cold and hopeless place
Similar to the planet called Pluto, that's up in space

Life in the ghetto is bitter, boring, and dark
Even on a sunny day it's no walk in the park

So if you live in a ghetto, then you know what I mean
We are the society, unfortunate and seldom seen

The days are numbered and time moves at a rapid pace
Living in the ghetto can be a winless race

This poem goes out to all the ghettos worldwide
God love us just the same, he's always by our side

THE LAST DAYS

The world is a time bomb waiting to explode
We're living in the last days so it's been told

There's no peace anywhere only rumors of war
The president wants Iraq to even the score

Sometimes I wonder if these days are cursed
Giving thanks to god for better or worst

This is the twentieth century what can we do
Violence has risen and nobody cares about you

People killing each other for no reason at all
Their expectations fail and they hit a brick wall

Our children suffer because of these careless acts
They lose the desire to achieve and fall off track

We must face each day with faith and hope
It's a tug of war that has a good and evil rope

THE LAST DEBATE

Well it's time for the last debate
Remembering things gone by that made you hate.

Remembering people that came between you and your family.
And you tried to right the wrong but no one seemed to see.

So all you have left is your pride.
And you're mean enough to hardly hide.

You tried hard, but maybe not enough
To over come the bull and stuff.

So now you figure it's no time to peeve
Pack up your stuff and get ready to leave.

You are not old, and have had your fill
So it's time to leave, and damn the bitter pill.

So let's say it's a matter of fate.
That's why this is called the last debate.

By the Late
Rudolph Lipsey Sr.

THE MIND, HEART, AND SPIRIT

Three major elements of the body are spirit, heart, and mind
Each one plays an important part at some point in time

The mind has to function, it stores information and creates
Controls your actions, directs and dictates

The heart is where the feeling of joy and pain
A place that pumps blood flow through your veins

Your spirit is filled with desires, hopes, and dreams
It's the strongest area of our physical being

Without these three assets we can't compete in life
Our spirit, heart, and mind similar to husband, children, and
wife

Each individual has a spirit, heart, and mind
Through God's grace and mercy their all one of a kind

THE STREETS

When you're out on the streets, prepare yourself at all times
There are no rules and regulations, only vicious violent crimes

The name of the game is called, playing for keeps
It's the first lesson you learn when hanging in the streets

You have to keep it real, and stand by your word
Cause on the streets nobody listens, just wants to be heard

On every street you have the corner, known as the block
Constant activity and major drug dealing around the clock

The stick-up man is always near by, waiting to strike
Out on the streets, he's the one, the hustlers totally dislike

If you can't hold your own on the streets, I suggest you stay inside
There's no where to run for cover or even a safe place to hide

They say the streets is where you learn about life and death
Each day you survive on the streets, is worth every breath

The streets are filled with bitterness, anger, and pain
Lives are constantly shattered and no one to take the blame

Making deals with the devil, while trying to out think the police
That's part of the mystery and insanity of living in the streets

Running from the fear of real life, leads you to the streets
But only God" can save your soul in the belly of the beast

This poem goes out to my comrades living in the streets day and night
The time will come, when the curtains close and on come the light

THE YOUTH OF TODAY

The youth of today are in need of love
We must teach them the word above

They will continue to struggle each day
Let's teach them to live in a godly way

Our youth must step up to the plate
Accepting their faults, failures, and mistakes

Sharing with them our experience and hope
Giving them the rules to learn the ropes

Time has come for parents to take a stand
Raising our children and not the hand

Every child should be treated the same
In order for them to learn the game

Each child has a special purpose on earth
That's why mothers are able to give birth

The youth of today are the youth of tomorrow
They are suffering in great pain and sorrow

If we don't take a stand today
Our youth will continue to fade away

THERE'S NO WAITING IN LINE

When your life is over and *God* calls you home
There's a voice you hear, that has a trumpet tone

Everyone has to take the same road
The doors are open and never closed

He will let you know the exact date and time
There's no need to rush there's no waiting in line

Understanding this process really makes sense
Because departing this life is no coincidence

We are just passing through, so enjoy the ride
They say that it's better on the other side

So for the time you're here, do your very best
God judges us all based on our final test

Live everyday with a humble state of mind
Always remember to be generous and kind

THINKING

Thinking can take you to a different place
Every mind that functions has thinking space

Thinking is very important when taking a chance
The outcome will be your thinking in advance

Thinking has a special place inside the mind
Everyone must think at some point in time

Thinking is definitely a Godly act
It's truly a blessing that thinking has such impact

Thinking will bring out your deepest thoughts
Your true inner thinking can't be sold or bought

Thinking enables you to focus and grow
Your thinking makes the choice of yes or no

The power of thinking can give you hope
Your thinking has a vision of a telescope

Thinking is open minded, honest and true
There's no way to separate thinking it's a part of you

THIS TIME

This time I will do better by giving my all
Even if I stumble, trip or take a fall

I know that this time God stands with me
So this time my mind is focused and now I can see

The last time I didn't try this time it's for real
Accepting the challenge and swallowing the bitter pill

This time the stakes are high there's no time out
I will play by the rules this time, casting all doubt

This time I'm going to be patient and take my time
By having faith and walking the straight line

This time could be my very last
Today I must face my fears and this time I will pass

TIME

There's not enough time to do all you can
Even with God's blessings and a master plan

The time we have is only for a short while
You must be willing and able to go the extra mile

Our time on this earth is truly a blessing
How you spend your time, is the important lesson

Time is everlasting, it will be forever more
We are given time, similar to a revolving door

The time will come and pass you by
We all must expect in time to die

Time is so important and precious today
Remember to take time to kneel and pray

You never know when your time will come
Prepare yourself in more ways than one

TIME IS PRECIOUS

Time is *precious*, cherish it to the end
It moves at a pace just like the wind

We all have a certain time on this earth
"God" grants us life, mothers give birth

So spend your time with great concern
The older you get the more you learn

Time will come and pass you by
There's a time to laugh and a time to cry

Time has no limitation and that's a fact
You must keep up with time to be exact

As you grow, the time starts to change
Some times are difficult and even strange

Time is forever and it's here to stay
I wish that it was more time, in a day

TO MY HONEY

"Honey" you are the reason why I'm serene today
I thank god for sending someone like you my way

The poetry and change, I did it for you and me
Without you, I don't know where I would be

When you read this poem, think about me, and you
The storms we weathered, but still made it through

All that I write, is dedicated to you, my one true love
We've come this far by faith, with blessing from above

So don't you worry about the past, it's nothing new
I will continue to make you happy in all that I do

This love affair and marriage is truly a gift of life
Two people who were meant to be, husband and wife

Honey I thank you for having my kids and standing by my side
You never gave up, despite at times the bumpy ride

Being with you, has made life worth living and totally complete
Your charming smile and pretty face will put a crying baby asleep

TRUST

It's very difficult to put your trust in someone or something. By the same token one day we'll have no choice. You have to first accept "GOD" into your "life" asking for his guidance and support. Trust is a very powerful word and at times, is taken for granted. In order to trust you must have a good "heart," that's where the main ingredient lies. Your heart will help you identify with untrustworthy situations, people, places, and things. You can't trust, all at once and it doesn't take years to develop trust, for example if you have a plant and you want it to develop, you have to put trust in watering it properly and making sure it gets treated daily in order for the plant to blossom. The same scenario applies to people. You have to be open-minded, willing, and tolerant. Conversation with an individual, sharing your time with them, you're practicing trust, getting to know certain things about them. However, you can't trust everyone, which is understandable. The key to embracing trust is trusting yourself and learning how to trust others.

TUPAC SHAKUR

He was a legend in his short time, the best pound for pound
His lyric's so powerful, awesome, and profound

Tupac was on top of his game in the rap world
He took rap hip hop to another level, a true black pearl

Out of all the rappers in the industry and worldwide
Not one possess Tupac's natural gift or even his pride

Machiavelli, keep your head up and all eyes on me
Only Tupac Shakur could share those words of history

He was truly the greatest rapper that ever lived life
Leaving this bitter and jealous world without a child or a wife

God blessed Tupac with the gift to rap and act
I know he made it to thug's mansion, and that's a fact

To his mother "Afeni" may your son Tupac rest in peace
His name and fame will travel the world, North, South, West,
and East

This poem goes out to Tupac Shakur, we miss you everyday
You will always be the one and only because you paved the
way

If you knew Tupac, I would suggest you take a bow
He is an icon, representing rap history in the here and now

TWO THOUSAND AND THREE

2003

Two thousand and three is the newest year
I am so happy and proud to be here

My goals for this year is to do Gods will
Facing life on its terms and keeping it real

Accepting the challenges, even defeat
Will only make me stronger instead of weak

I know that determination and faith is the key
Because in 2002 God showed me

I want to start this New Year on the right track
Only to remember the past without looking back

That year is gone and over, I made it through
It's time to move on there's nothing else to do

As the New Year gets moving I hope and pray
For peace on earth each and everyday

In 2003 I will be patient and take my time
Enjoy life to the fullest with an open mind

UNITED RAPPERS OF AMERICA

The rap world is full of trouble, suspense, and lost fame
Tupac and Biggie were soldiers true to the game

Why can't we rap without using harsh words
Beefing with one another is negative and absurd

Shady records and Murder Inc. should sit down and talk
Name calling, making public threats, man take a walk

There's nothing wrong with a rivalry just keep it clean
Everybody is making the cheddar while living out their dream

We've come to far let's live and have big fun
Enjoying the finer things in life that's how it should be done

The rap industry is where we make our bread and butter
Majority of the talent shared came from the ghetto gutter

What's the purpose of rapping if you can't see it manifest
Watching your back at all cost and wearing a bullet proof vest

Look what happened to legend Jam Master Jay
The killer is still at large he didn't have to go out that way

It's time to come together and make our ancestors smile
They are the original creators of the Rap and Hip Hop style

Dmx, Jarule, Fifty Cents just to name a few young rap stars
There's over two million black men lock down behind bars

We should learn a lesson from the past and live for today
Hip Hop and Rap will go on forever because it's here to stay

UNITED STATES POSTAL SERVICE

The U.S. postal service America's finest workforce
They are the life line and primary resource

The staff consists of carriers, processors, handlers, and clerks
Each dept. has a postmaster and supervisors who dictate the work

Without the postal service there's no way to send or receive mail
It's an around the clock effort to please their clientele

The U.S. postal service has been around for many years
We must give our organization, praise, respect, and cheers

I am part of the postal service and proud to be
Because it represents the land of the brave home of the free

The postal service and staff deserve an award for who we are
Giving the world our all while shining like a star

The postal service prayers go out to the families of nine one-one
And those who participated in ground zero for a job well done

WHEN I GET TO HEAVEN

When I get to heaven and God calls my name
I will give up my past, fortune, and fame

I will be patient while on earth and wait my turn
Because making it to heaven is my greatest concern

As I prepare myself by doing the right things
I can imagine the joy of going to heaven brings

Living my life in this body of a shell
Defines the true essence of heaven over hell

There's a difference between heaven and earth
Heaven is home your spiritual place of birth

So when I get to heaven the pain and sorrow will end
No longer will I have to live through the hate and sin

WHEN *I* OPEN *MY* EYES

When I open up my bright eyes there is a lot of positive things that I see. When I open my eyes life is so beautiful, my future becomes so clear. The world starts to turn, and God's blessings upon me are here. Just by opening up my eyes alerts my mind to acknowledge my vision, my life, and myself. I've come to realize how much joy and love I inherit when I open my eyes. When I wake up in the morning and the sunlight greets my eyes all I can do is thank God. I have learned a valuable lesson in and throughout my life, in order to capitalize on your perspective of living a comfortable and content life; I must accept Jesus Christ my savior because without that faith there's no hope. Last but not least just simply open up my eyes.

WHERE I GREW UP

Where I grew up there was no doctors, lawyers, or writers
All I saw were drug addicts, dealers, whore's and prize fighters

Where I grew up education consisted of your street skills of
knowledge
Your goals and dreams didn't exist I never thought of college

Where I grew up times were hard only the strong would survive
The average life expectancy was ten to twenty five

Where I grew up I lived everyday as if it was the last
The neighborhoods were full of trouble, crime was first class

Where I grew up poverty was at an all time high
Welfare public assistance is how the family got by

Where I grew up most families were single parent homes
The majority headed by firm mother's who often held their own

Where I grew up was often filled with pain and sorrow
Going to sleep at night while praying for tomorrow

Where I grew up I wish, hope, and dream
That one day I would be able to accomplish almost anything

WINNING

In the game of life winning is the key to success
Playing by the rules you're bound to pass the test

You must step up to the plate when it's your turn
Accepting the challenge enables you to win and learn

Sometimes you have to lose in order to win
The reward comes from your desire at the end

Winning consist of practice and working hard
When you compete you earn a winning card

Winning gives you inspiration and that's what it takes
By pushing yourself to the limit will open the gate

Winning is the compensation of every game you lost
Give God all praise for guiding you and paying the cost

WORLD OF TROUBLE

We are living in troubled times
People committing vicious crimes

The house of congress has voted war
Our children are dying like never before

The years pass by at a rapid pace
There's even a new planet up in space

I ask god to give me strength each day
And hope that tomorrow comes my way

This world has endured so much pain
Watching the twin towers go down in flames

I wonder if the world is coming to an end
Or could it be evil acts by wicked men

The sniper situation makes matters worst
It's a world of trouble with a curse

WOULD YOU BE MINE

When we first met I knew you were the one
Your sexy charm, warm smile was bright as the sun

I can't wait to spend some quality time with you
We can take in a movie or perhaps a dinner for two

You and I could share the gift of life
Grow together and become husband and wife

Give me the opportunity in time you will see
I will take you places only meant for you and me

Please don't hesitate or make me wait too long
I promise never to hurt you or do you wrong

It's up to you I will meet your every need
This could be a beautiful flower if we plant the seed

I share this poem with someone that's special and kind
Because true love can be hard to find

You are my glass of water so fresh and clear
Would you please be mine there's nothing to fear

YEARS

Years are filled with love, peace, and pain
God has blessed us so why complain

Every year will be different from the last
We must live for today only to remember our past

This year is the most important year in your life today
Because the next year isn't promised to you anyway

When the years go by time starts to pick up pace
You must be mentally strong to finish the race

Years, they come and go like days and nights
Over the years you see so many stars shining bright

The number of years is only a few
It's written in the Holy Scriptures the old and new

YOU AND I

*L*ast night I went to sleep thinking about you
My thoughts were, kind, honest, and true

I know that you and I are meant to be
We share a special bond a blind man can see

Even though we may disagree at times
Our love for one another is pure and divine

Nothing in this world can break us apart
God has truly mended our two hearts

This love affair has all the natural ingredients
Two people who are honorable and obedient

By giving their all keeps the love pure and strong
Understanding one another whether right or wrong

I dedicate this poem to you for being my wife
You have made everything complete in my life

SAMIRA   *MANISA*

TAQUAN

MY THREE ANGLES

BROTHER RUDOLPH

Years ago when we first met
We didn't have a clue
How what we felt was family
Was bound to blossom too
Life wasn't warm and fuzzy, but
We took it stride by stride
Still it turned out to be one
Hell bent roller coaster ride
But through gods love and mercy
We've grown to love and cope
And witness friends and relatives
Abandon dreams and hope
I thank god for Brother Rudolph, and the
Love he gives to me
He is a pure example of what I call family

HASSAN THE POET

TO THE GREAT POETS BEFORE
MY TIME LANGSTON, ANGELOU,
GIOVANNI, BARAKA, AND
MORRISON
JUST TO NAME A FEW

RUDOLPH LIPSEY JR.

**FOR MORE INFORMATION
CONTACT: UPLIFTING POEMS FOR TROUBLED
HEARTS
P.O. BOX 13155
JERSEY CITY NJ. 07303**